IMAGES
of America

LEWISTON
AND
AUBURN

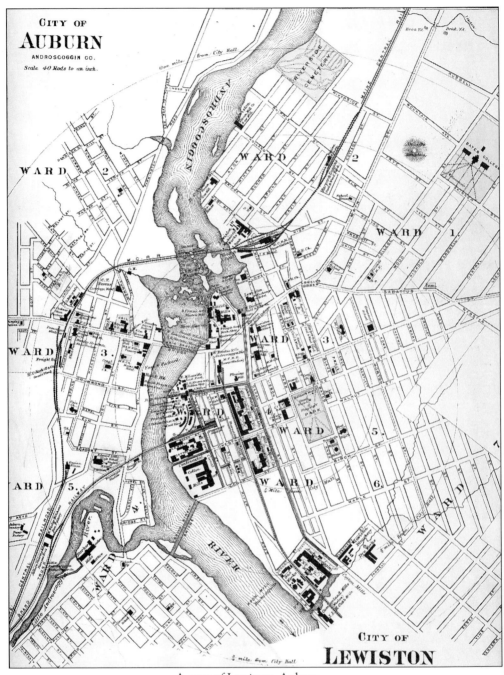

A map of Lewiston-Auburn.

IMAGES
of America

LEWISTON
AND
AUBURN

Reverend H. Kenneth Dutille

ARCADIA

First published 1995
Copyright © Reverend H. Kenneth Dutille, 1995

ISBN 0-7524-0220-X

Published by Arcadia Publishing,
an imprint of the Chalford Publishing Corporation
One Washington Center, Dover, New Hampshire 03820
Printed in Great Britain

Library of Congress Cataloging-in-Publication Data applied for

The interior of F.X. Marcotte, early 1900s. Founded in 1888, the original business, F.X. Marcotte, Undertaker and Dealer in Furniture and Stoves, was more of a general store. Today, F.X. Marcotte Furniture continues to be owned by descendants of the Marcotte family. (Photograph and information from The Franco-American Work Experience, L.A. College)

Contents

David Rowe's Livery Stable, Park Street, Lewiston. The brick building on the right was later destroyed.

Fred Morton and his two "vehicles." I wonder who won the race?

Introduction

I have tried to prepare *Lewiston and Auburn* so that it will be of pertinent interest and value not only to the citizens of Lewiston, Auburn, and Androscoggin County, but to other folks who are interested in the Twin Cities.

The period covered in this book goes from the pre-Civil War to the 1950s, with a few modern photographs. The 1900s Publicity Bureau (with A.L. Kavanagh as the director) reported the following about Lewiston and Auburn: "good salmon, and trout fishing, the purest water supplied through the best municipal water system in New England . . . very low tax rate . . . four National Banks . . . center of 170 miles of electric Roads . . . Lewiston, Augusta and Waterville Street Railway . . . 600 passenger cars head of Lisbon Street daily . . . Half hour services by electrics to Waterville via. Gardiner and Augusta; Bath via. Brunswick . . . three divisions Maine Central Railroad . . . several Express Trains daily east to west . . . Grand Trunk Railroad for the Canada's and West . . . one dozen express companies."

Have you ever wondered where the name "Androscoggin River" came from? The river divides Lewiston and Auburn. The *History of Androscoggin County* gives us some interesting ideas: "Androscoggin, according to one authority, comes from the Algonguin, the turbid, foaming, crocked snake. This later became Amerascoggin, Amoscoggin and Androscoggin. Captain John Smith in 1614 called the river Aumouchawgan. Another authority derives Amoscoggin from "namaes," meaning fish or spearing-fishing. Others still say Amoscoggin means "fish coming in the spring." The name of the river, Androscoggin, was early applied to the Anasagunticook Indians, whose headquarters at that time were in this valley."

The river runs about 166 miles in length. During the late 1890s the following manufacturing firms used water from the Androscoggin River for their power: the Bates Mill, the Hill Company, Androscoggin Mills, Continental Mills, Franklin Mills, Lewiston Mills, and the Lewiston Falls Manufacturing Company.

Androscoggin County separated from Cumberland, Oxford, Kennebec, and Lincoln County in 1854. On August 18, 1862, men from Lewiston and Auburn were included in the 17th Maine Infantry. The infantry took part in the Battles of Fredericksburg, Chancellorsville, and the famous Battle of Gettysburg.

Photographs have illuminated human history since their development, and they have recorded the history of the Twin Cities. They show us people, young and old, and have recorded for us a great deal of social history. Photographs are like windows in a house; they give us a view into our past. They are the buggy we ride as we view the human landscape of Lewiston and Auburn.

PROCLAMATION !

In view of the fact that for the four last days between the hours of four and eight in the afternoon, our streets have been full of crowds of people, creating a great tumult indicating and threatening a mob, and a breach of, and resistance to the laws of the State for the preservation of the peace and good order of our city. And that violence to persons has been committed ; therefore I request all persons to refrain from being upon the streets of the city, between the hours named except for necessary and proper purposes.

All persons found upon the streets in large or small crowds, and in any way participating in causing any disturbance or tumult, or contributing thereto, will be subject to arrest and punishment.

W. W. BOLSTER, MAYOR.

City of Auburn, Oct. 4, 1893.

A proclamation by Auburn's Mayor, W.W. Bolster, dated October 4, 1893.

One
Auburn: Court and Turner Streets

The Dillingham and Sons Funeral Parlor, 62–64 Spring Street (next to the old Auburn Fire Station). This was the first building they had. They had two private telephone lines numbers: 545 and 546. Their advertising said "We go anywhere—day or night." The funeral coach doubled as an ambulance.

The F.W. Adams Lumber Yard, 101 Turner Street, Auburn. A sign says "American Seal White Lead" sold here.

Ruggles Block, Auburn, at the north corner of Turner and Summer Street. This building is still standing, but was partly destroyed by fire. This picture was probably taken *c.* 1900. Note the carbon light on the tall street pole

The S.A. Pollister Store on 88 Court Street, Auburn. A sign near the door says "STOP! LOOK! BUY! The Ladies Home Journal." Sewall Pollister founded the store to sell rubber stamps, office supplies, newspapers, books, and magazines. S.A. Pollister was near the site of the new Orphan Annie's Store.

Court and Turner Streets, Auburn. The stores include Frank L. Beals (who sold fruit and confectioneries), S.A. Pollister, High Street Laundry, and the old Heath House. This photograph was taken *c*. 1898–1900. (Photograph by A.L. Robinson.)

The Androscoggin County Building, Auburn. This is an early photograph, because the Statue and Court Street Baptist are not pictured here. (Photograph by R. Dresser.)

Court and Turner Streets, Auburn. Note the old Libby Bakery, the trolley car heading over the Androscoggin River, Flanders Store (on the right), and the wooden boxes of Moxie in front of the store on the left.

A soldier's funeral procession in 1919, across from the Androscoggin County Courthouse. There is an American flag over the casket. Notice the cobble stones on the street. The soldier was Alden M. Gayton, who was the first person from Auburn to die in World War I. American Legion Post #31 is named after him. (Photograph by Houle.)

Seaveys of Auburn served up some of the greatest ice cream floats in the area. This was also the bus terminal for the Maine Central Bus Service. It was located on the corner of Minot Avenue and Court Street where the Union Street bypass was. Note the trolley car tracks.

Two

Lewiston: Lisbon and Main Streets

The William H. Bailey Cobbler Shop, 218 Main Street, Lewiston. The Wing Chung Laundry was located on the right. The sign on the left says "Greatest Bargains in Harnesses ever offered in Lewiston." The building on the far right was the J. Curtis Livery Stable. This photograph was taken in 1896. (Photograph by Poisson.)

Lisbon Street from Pine Street looking towards Main Street. The following store fronts can be seen on the left side: Bradford, Conant & Company, Sam'L Hibbert's Oyster Eating House, Chas. Greenwood Stoves, the American Express Company, and the International Express Company. On the right side you can see Ricker's Apothecary and Manufacturers National Bank.

The Munroe Building, 215 Lisbon Street, Lewiston. The Lewiston Rubber Company was on the first floor on the right. Their sign says "The House that gives you more rubber for a Dollar." They sold elastic stockings, belts, and water bottles. The next stores are Meltzer, LE Messager, and Berube's Cafe. On the second floor were located the M.J. Hagerty Fire Insurance Co., Williams Law Office, Pelletier's Beauty Parlor, the P.E. Tremblay Law Office, H.E. Belleau, and Robert College. Across the street on the right was Bradford Conant and Company Furniture. Note the trolley tracks on Lisbon Street. (Photograph by Harry L. Plummer.)

L.L. Blake and Company, 155 Lisbon Street, Lewiston. The company float was all ready to join the 1910 parade. Note the cobblestones that were used for paving the streets. L.L. Blake and Company sold furniture, carpets, and draperies. Notice the little American flag on the horse's ear. A gentleman is looking out the second-story window, probably giving some last minute suggestions for the float.

The Chabot and Richard Company, 162–166 Lisbon Street, Lewiston. Advertising on the postcard states "The Fastest growing Dry and Fancy Goods House in the City. It is with great pleasure that we announce our GRAND OPENING of Paris Model Hats and Creations for our own work rooms. We will display also the latest in suits, furs, skirts, shirt waists, silks, dress goods, belts, neckwear and trimmings. Your attendance is solicited. Music afternoon and evening." This fine store was located in the McGillicuddy Building. M. Willaim Richard founded the store in 1903, and built it into the largest of its kind in the state. He changed the name in 1917 to Richard's Exclusive Shops, and opened one in Waterville on Main Street in the Cyr Building. Richard was one of the founders of B. Peck and Company.

The Boston Shoe Store, 113 Lisbon Street, Lewiston. The card states "Latest, Largest and Finest stock of boots and shoes in the state, Sign of the Golden Slipper."

The Great Blizzard of 1888, Lisbon Street, Lewiston. The trolley tracks are being plowed by a #7 rotary plow manufactured by the Peckham Truck Company, Kingston, New York. Notice the store signs advertising the J.H. Stetson Co., Crawford Ranges, and the Knight Hardware Co.

The Great Blizzard of 1888, Lisbon Street from Ash Street looking toward Main Street. The following store fronts can be seen: Curtis & Ross Photographers & Job Printing, John Hibbert's Lunch and Oyster House, the Beaver Drug Store, the Stanley Co., and Osward and Armstrong. The Osward and Armstrong Store was a dry and fancy goods dealer. They were the successors of the Arthur Sand Store, and they owned five stores on Lisbon Street.

The kitchen of Hibbert's Restaurant, 195 Lisbon Street, Lewiston. From left to right are Mrs. Hibbert, Tilly McCormick, Mrs. Goss, and Mary Dorscall. A Fairbanks "gold dust" baking powder box can be seen on a shelf. (The Thompson Photo Co.)

The front dining room of Hibbert's Restaurant, Lewiston. Notice the deer head mounted on the wall.

Sam Hibbert's Eating House, 195 Lisbon Street, Lewiston, 1898. Sam Hibbert lived up over the restaurant. He was the father of William G. Hibbert, later the cashier of the First National Bank, Lewiston. On the right window is a large poster which says "$3,500.00 The Central Maine Circuit: Lewiston Fairfield & Augusta, RACES EACH DAY."

Judkins Laundry, 187 Lisbon Street, Lewiston. Mr. Everett A. Davis is on the right. Judkins was one of the oldest launderers in the Twin Cities. Judkins Laundry merged in 1963 with Auburn's Norris-Hayden Company, and Modern Cleaners. Their new name was Associated Laundries. The sign on the right of the photograph says "M.N. Frye Dress & J Clock Maker."

The Daniel Doyle Store on 38 Lisbon Street, Lewiston, as it looked in 1900. This establishment sold crockery, glassware, china, and lamps. There is a sign in the window that says "rooms to lend." Next door is Tainter's Music Store.

Babcock and Sharp's Drug Store, Lisbon Street, Lewiston. Idell Blaisdell is on the right. On the left is a calendar from the New England Mutual Insurance Company; the date is Tuesday, June 12. The wall clock on the left was made by Standard Time, and the time is 9:25. The sun is shining through the front window from Lisbon Street so it has to be in the morning. All flavors of ice cream soda could be bought for 10¢. In the middle of the picture is a container of Welch's Grape Juice. The cash register was manufactured by National. Notice the bowl with lemons and limes on the counter. Many young people in the Twin Cities had their first date at Babcock and Sharp's Drug Store.

Main Street, Lewiston, near the corner of Park Street. This photograph includes the Main Street Bakery, Jordan's Store (which sold tea, coffee, butter, and eggs), and the Union Market.

The Kora Temple, Main Street, Lewiston. Chartered by the Imperial Council in 1891, their first meeting place was next to the old New England Furniture building on Lisbon Street. Francis T. Faulkner was the first potentate. The temple was finished in 1909.

The First Baptist Church (Calvinist Baptist), corner of Main and Lisbon, Lewiston. The church cost about $10,000 to build in 1853. The church's first minister, Reverend George Knox, was killed during the Civil War when he was thrown from a horse. In 1978 the building caught on fire, but it was rebuilt inside and is known today as the Gateway Building.

Three
Entertaining Our People

Looking towards the corner of Bates and Pine Street, the Young Men's Christian Association can be seen at the upper left. A Baptist church (left) is in the distance. It looks like it was a beautiful day for a parade. From left to right are Mary Pottle, unknown, Lucy Craig Parker, unknown, unknown, and Christine Gerrish (a druggist on Lisbon Street, Lewiston). The group is located at the City Park. In 1861 the Franklin Company gave 8 acres in front of their DeWitt Hotel to the City of Lewiston to be used for a park.

The Ringling Brothers Circus, June 10, 1911, Main and Sabattus Streets, Lewiston. Notice the signs advertising A.E. Harlow Candy Company, Caskets. (Photograph by G. Herbert Whitney.)

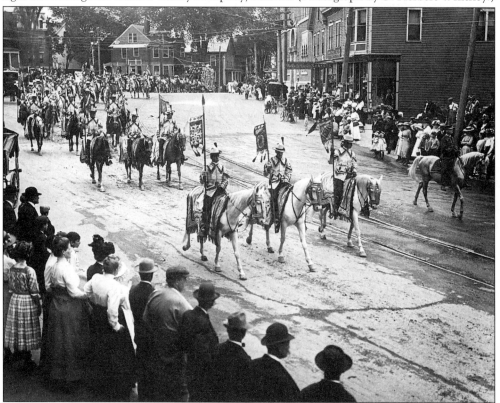

Buffalo Bill's Circus, June 3, 1911, Lewiston. This was the tent where the meals were prepared.

✳ DRAMATIC ✳

ENTERTAINMENT

AT ENGINE HALL,

SATURDAY EVE., MARCH 2, '89

At which time will be presented the interesting Drama.

"ENLISTED FOR THE WAR"

CAST OF CHARACTERS:

ROBERT TRUEWORTH,	Mr. CAROL BAILEY
WILDER ROWELL,	Mr. CHAS. BAILEY
HOSEA JENKS,	Mr. FRANK MERRILL
HIRAM JENKS,	Mr. HIRAM BRIGGS
CRIMP, (colored),	Mr. C. H. BAILEY
GENERAL GRANT,	Mr. T. A. BAILEY
LIEUT. COL. BOXER,	Mr. O. E. JOHNSON
GAYLIE GIFFORD,	Miss SADIE CLOUGH
Mrs. TRUEWORTH,	Mrs. MAY WHITMAN
MATTIE TRUEWORTH.	Miss EDITH OSGOOD

SYNOPSIS.

ACT. 1st. The old farm sold. Hosea Jenk's very funny puns. Robert Trueworth enlists
ACT. 2d. Crimp loses his pass. Gen. Grant abandons his cigar and Robert Trueworth finds
a friend.
ACT. 3d. The war is over. Jenks loses his mirth for a time but it returns again. Robert
Trueworth comes home promoted, and Col. Rowell gets demoralized.

GOOD MUSIC IN ATTENDANCE.

ADMISSION, 15 Cts.   CHILDREN, under 12, 10 Cts.

Doors open at 6:30 o'clock.   Curtain at 7:30 o'clock.

DRAMATIC!!! The Universalist Social Circle of North Auburn gave a DRAMATIC
ENTERTAINMENT at Engine Hall, on Saturday evening, March 2, 1889. It must have been
quite an evening with the presentation of the drama *Enlisted For The War*: Act 1 featured the
old farm being sold, Hosea Jenk's very funny puns, and the enlistment of Robert Trueworth; in
Act 2 Crimp loses his pass, General Grant abandons his cigar, and Robert Trueworth finds a
friend; and in Act 3 the war ends, Jenks loses his mirth for a time but it returns again, Robert
Trueworth comes home promoted, and Colonel Rowell gets demoralized. Admission for all this
was only 15¢.

This is how the corner of Ash and Lisbon Streets looked in 1899 during a parade. The photograph was taken looking south down on Lisbon Street. Note the pair of horses (right) probably pulling a horse car. On the left is the "Blue Store" advertised as "Lewiston's Largest Clothing House." The Blue Store started in 1880, and it was sold to the Low-King Company of Portland in 1909. Notice the carbon street lights. On the right side of the street from left to right were the following businesses: Health & Tainter Coal, a laundry, Lemont & Fisher, Atwood's Market, L.L. Blake Furniture, Daniel Wood, and the YMCA Free Reading Room.

Company "C," Auburn Light Infantry, May 2, 1898. The Russ Bradbury Livery Stable is on the left on the river bank. Later they did business as Libby and Pellengill. On the right is the Auburn Cigar store. (Photograph by A.L. Robinson.)

The Forepaugh and Sells Circus, July 3–4, 1910, Lewiston. This was the cooking tent.

This 1876 stereo view card shows Charles Hilton, a tight rope walker, on a high wire over the Androscoggin River. That, I bet, would draw quite a group of people. (Photographed and published by C.B. Conant, Lewiston.)

The Kiwanians are putting up playground equipment for the playground on Lincoln Street, Lewiston. This 1922 photograph includes Dr. George F. Finnie (pastor of the United Baptist Church, Main Street, Lewiston), Dr. A.N. Leonard (of the Bates College facility), and Elmer L. Briggs (real estate and insurance broker of Auburn).

The famous William R. Chapman was the director-in-chief of the Maine Music Festival in the early 1920s (he was also invloved in the New York Philharmonic Society Chorus of three hundred voices). The headquarters of the festival was Tainter's Music Store, 40–42 Lisbon Street, Lewiston. The "Hallelujah Chorus" was to be sung at every festival. Arthur G. Staples wrote in the official souvenir program from October 5–6, 1925, that "This is the third music festival in Lewiston, distinctively the Festival of the Valley of the Androscoggin. Bangor has her festival, and the Valley of the Androscoggin now has hers. Let us not believe for a moment that the Maine Festival at Lewiston is merely an entertainment. It is an educational school in its happiest form, an uplift, a call to service." Seldon T. Craft was president of the festival; the vice-president was Juanita William, and Dana Rowe was treasurer.

Mr. Darling of Darling Auto Sales, Auburn, and company enjoy an outing at Darling's Farm on Taylor Pond. This outing was held in the summer of 1919 and was most likely a company picnic. Darling Auto Sales was one of the first companies to sell autos in the Twin Cities. The firm was located on Franklin Street, Auburn, near the old post office.

The Industry Lodge #2 Knights of Pythias and Miller's Cornet Band, Lewiston. The band is at the corner of Court and North Main Street, Auburn. Note Elm House, the Auburn Clothing House, and Sykes and Howe Clothiers.

The Auburn Drum Corp. The Lewiston-Auburn Falls is in the background. The photograph was taken from the Auburn side. The buildings on Island Garden are to the upper right. These ten boys got together during the summer of 1892 for this photograph session.

The King Brothers Circus, June 30, 1948, Lewiston.

The King Brothers and Cristiani Circus, June 17, 1952, Lewiston. The circus grounds were just off Central Avenue, beyond Russell Street. (Photograph by G. Herbert Whitney.)

The King Brothers and Cristiani Circus, June 17, 1952, Lewiston. The calliope at the circus grounds, off Central Avenue, was originally in the old Gentry Bros. circus, 1903. (Photograph by G. Herbert Whitney.)

The King Brothers and Cristiani Circus, June 17, 1952, Lewiston. "HUGO ZACCHINI" was the Human Cannon Ball, and was shot up to 330 feet through the air. (Photograph by G. Herbert Whitney.)

Barnum and Bailey's "Greatest Show on Earth" played to thousands when it was in Lewiston. This unique photograph was advertising the Waterville show which Barnum and Bailey would perform when they were in the Lewiston area. They used fifty performing horses in a single act, and would advertise the "show" on buildings.

The Barnum and Bailey Circus, 1918. This was the cooking tent.

The year 1895 was important in the history of Lewiston, because it saw the St. Dominique Band organized. Two early band leaders were William Given and Louis N. Gendreau.

The grandstand on the Maine State Fair Grounds, Lewiston.

The Maine State Fair, Lewiston. Do you see the team of oxen pulling the very heavy looking load? If you look at the upper left hand corner you will notice the exhibition hall, which was a three-story building.

These cottages were on the Lewiston Fairgrounds. Note the "period" hats and dresses that the ladies have on. People would rent these cottages for the week when they were attending the Lewiston Fairgrounds. The fair was at one time the state's largest.

These very talented boys from Lewiston formed the "Lewiston Boys Band" (the St. Cecilia Band). They performed not only in Lewiston, but also toured in Canada. They played for fifty years. You could hear them in the summer months at Old Orchard, and they also played at the Poland Springs Inn. The band was founded in 1894 by the Dominican Fathers. They appointed Brother Aymond as director, but he was transferred to a monastery in Europe early during his directorship.

Entrance to Lake Grove Park, Auburn Lake, Auburn, Me.

The entrance to Lake Grove Park, Lake Auburn, Auburn. As you entered the park, you would go through large stone pillars, which always had beautiful flowers on their top. Lake Grove Park closed in the early 1900s after the Twin Cities decided to get their drinking water from Lake Auburn.

Lake Grove, Auburn. People from the Twin Cities would travel by trolley during the hot summer days to Lake Grove, where they would enjoy the theater or have a picnic under the tall trees. After a day here you would feel refreshed.

The Lake Grove House, East Auburn. This hotel offered accommodations for weary travelers. The entire area around the Lake Grove House offered a great time for everyone.

The Lake Grove Horsecar at the corner of Court and Goff Streets. This was the first "car" powered by horses that ran between Lewiston and Lake Grove. You might remember Fred Bird of Auburn who drove the "car" between Lewiston and Lake Grove. It ran on tracks except during Maine's cold winters, when it was put on runners.

Androscoggin Rail Road.

State Fair Week, Special Trains Will Run as Follows:

Tuesday, Wednesday, Thursday & Friday, Sep. 20, 21, 22 & 23.

Leave Farmington at 5 A. M., East Wilton, 5.15, Wilton, 5.25, N. Jay, 5.35, Jay Bridge 5.45, Livermore Falls 5.55, East Livermore 6.10, Strickland's Ferry 6.20, North Leeds 6.30, Leeds Center 6.38, Curtis Corner 6.45, Leeds Crossing 7.00, Sabattis 7.20, **Lewiston** 7.20, Crowley's 7.35, Lisbon 7.45, Lisbon Falls 7.55. Arrive at Brunswick 8.20.

Returning, leave Brunswick at 4.45 P. M.,

These Special Trains will keep clear of all Regular Passenger Trains. Freight and Gravel Trains will keep clear of these Special Trains.

ARTHUR BROWN, Supt.

Farmington, Sept. 19th, 1870.

"Special" trains featured in the Androscoggin Railroad State Fair Week. These trains "kept clear" of all regular passenger trains (as freight and gravel trains kept clear of the special trains). Arthur Brown was the superintendent when this notice was dated: September 19, 1879.

Four

The Androscoggin River: Floods, Ferries, and Fun

This photograph was taken on the corner of Court and Main Streets, Auburn, during the big Flood of 1936. Well-known Auburn citizens are sizing up the situation: standing, from left to right, are Horace Edward Munroe, John Merrill, and John Cartwright.

This photograph shows the Androscoggin River hitting the North Bridge between Auburn and Lewiston. The North Bridge withstood the flood, but the South Bridge wasn't as fortunate.

The Grand Trunk Railroad Bridge during the Flood of 1936 had many people taking pictures.

Miller Street, Auburn, during the 1936 Flood.
The Grand Trunk Railroad Bridge can be seen in
the far background.

Miller Street at the rear of Court Street, Auburn,
during the March 1936 Flood.

Roak's Greenhouse was located at the time of the 1936 Flood in the "Hollow" beside the Edward Little High School, Auburn.

The Maine Central Railroad Bridge over the Androscoggin River, from the Auburn side.

The North Bridge before the Flood of 1896. This picture was taken from the Lewiston side looking towards Auburn. Notice on the Lewiston side the following store signs: Pond's Extract, Hodgkins, Foss & Company, and Job Carpenter & Builders (dealers in doors, windows, and blinds). The old Lewiston City Hall is on the right. Note the tower. (E.E. Sturtevant Portrait and View Artists, Auburn.)

The North Bridge after the Flood of 1896. (Photograph by E.E. Sturtevant.)

The North Bridge, 1890s, looking from Lewiston toward Auburn. Note the signs advertising Saw Filing, Wilson ? and Company, and the Steam Bakery. The Androscoggin County Building and the steeple from the Court Street Baptist Church can also be seen.

The Littlefield Corner Bridge, over the Little Androscoggin River, on the Old Hotel Road, Auburn.

A side view of the South Bridge over the Androscoggin River looking from the Auburn side.

Workmen laying the water line above Lewiston Falls on the Androscoggin River.

The Auburn Ice House above the dam. Because Maine's winters were so cold, harvesting and selling of ice became a large business. This photograph of men cutting the ice is dated 1913. The Auburn Crystal Ice Company operated in the Twin Cities for fifty years. They operated an ice house near Lake Auburn, and another one on Avon Street, Lewiston. They made home deliveries. They would cut the ice from Lake Auburn and the Androscoggin River. Oliver Newman and Daniel Lara started the company, then sold the firm to a partnership made up of the Bearce and Wilson families. E.P. Langley eventually owned the company, but the last owner was Wesley Urquhart. Maine had one of the largest ice manufacturing businesses in the eastern half of the United States.

Skating on the Androscoggin River between the Twin Cities.

The South Ferry, established to make travel between Lewiston and Auburn easier after the Flood of 1896. The stone piers of the defunct South Bridge can be seen in the distance. One of the wagons on the ferry says ? and Tea Company.

The Gulf Island Dam. Notice the work being done by horses in the above photograph. It took two years to construct the dam. Many men worked twelve-hour days, seven days a week. A special railroad line was laid from the town of Leeds, (where the gravel deposit was located), along Switzerland Road to the Island project. Over 11,000 cubic yards of rock was blasted and nearly one million yards of cement were poured.

Five

The Twin Cities in Business and Manufacturing

Whitco Building Materials. Now that is quite a mobile billboard. This is the J.W. White Lumber Company (the telephone number was 330). The firm was located on Lincoln Street, Lewiston, where the Atlas Supply Company is today. During the Flood of 1936 much damage was done to the White Lumber Company. This house-auto was very popular during parades in the Twin Cities. (Photograph by Harry Plummer.)

The R.C. Pingree and Company Wood Working Shop. W.L. Davis was the superintendent. The lumber mill was located on the banks of the Androscoggin River, just above Lewiston's Falls. The company was formed as the S.R. Beace Company in 1865. Steam engines turned out millions of board feet of lumber in the many years that the mill operated. Pingree employed about one hundred people at its peak.

Steven's Tank and Tower, Center Street, Auburn. Notice the amount of snow that fell that winter.

The interior of the Paradis and Leblanc Store, 184–188 Lisbon Street, Lewiston. Henry N. Paradis and Gerald R. Leblanc opened their store in January 1946, on the site of the former John B. St. Pierre men's store. They had an earlier store called The Men's Store at 272–274 Lisbon Street. Previous to that, Paradis had a men's store in partnership with Roland Faucher. (From the Franco-American Heritage Collection, L.A. College.)

Clifton White's 2-and-1/2-H.P. sawing outfit. This "old" machine kept many houses warm in Lewiston during the cold winter months.

The Plummer C. Tarbox Flour Company of Lewiston. This unique stereo view card shows the flour wagons ready to make a delivery. Next door to Tarbox Flour was the Bagley and Clark Market and the C.J. Bolton Grocery Store.

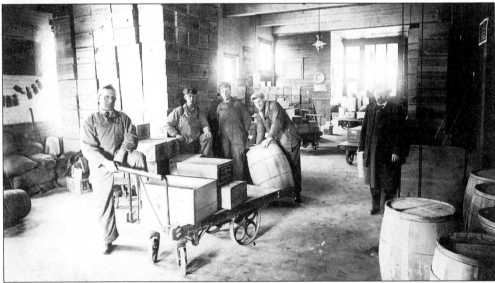

The F.G. Davis Wholesale Grocery Store, Lewiston. Henry Bradford is on the far left, and George Curtis is on the far right with the suit on. The wooden boxes on the left are marked "tomatoes," while the wooden boxes on the back wall have glass bottles of "Moxie" in them. Freeman George Davis owned the company. Freeman "possessed an altruistic mentality that made him popular in all circles and was called the voice of the electorate as its representative" (*A History of Maine*). Originally, the firm included a Mr. Curtis and a Mr. Record. Davis was known for reinvesting his profits back in the company. He was a director and vice-president of the First Auburn Trust Company, and a member of the High Street Congregational Church (Auburn), the Republican Party, the Kiwanis Club, the Independent Order of Odd Fellows, and was a 32-degree Mason. He died on a business trip to California at the age of sixty-four.

The J.E. Tibbetts Company. This photograph was taken in 1895, and the business was located at 163 Turner Street, Auburn. It was located north of the railroad overpass. Tibbetts was an agent for the William Tell Flour Company, and sold flour, grain, feed, and hay. Notice the horse and wagons making their daily deliveries. (Photograph by Ernest Mason, Auburn.)

In eight minutes or less you could get your car's oil changed. The Bell Tire Company was open twenty-four hours a day because the Bell's wanted to give the kind of service that people wanted. In his advertisements Bell would say "I value your time and I don't keep you standing around waiting. It's all business and quick pleasing service at my farm." He goes on to say, "I have tried to give better service than anybody else and as a result I've been able to keep in business, pay my bills, buy the wife a fur coat, send Danny, Irving, and Lester to school, and to keep all of them plump and happy." The station was located above the fairground.

Bell says "Meet the family, they've all got an interest in the business, cause no business, no eats, and you can judge by the picture whether business has been good or bad, and yes folks the raccoon has been paid for—the last installment paid last month—THANK GOD." The Bell Oil Company, one of Maine's largest dealers, had gasoline and oil tanks on the Lewiston Railroad siding capable of holding 140,000 gallons.

58

Crowley's Flower Farm, on Lisbon Road (near the old Lisbon Drive-In), was owned by Harry and Florence Crowley. Harry was a former Maine state senator and insurance agent. Note the lighthouse and small fish pond. The pond had goldfish in it and during the winter months the goldfish would live in a small pool under a flower bench in the greenhouse.

This brick shoe factory building was built in 1873, and was reported to have been 122 feet long and 40 feet wide with five floors. The company was owned by E.F. Packard and B.F. Briggs. Like so many of the factories of this time it used steam power to run the many machines. It was noted in *Androscoggin County History* (1891) that there were some 6,000 pairs of womens' and misses' boots and shoes produced. At the time this picture was taken in the early 1880s, the I.C. Lombard Company had moved into one section of the building. This company began in 1864 on Goff Hill, Auburn, opposite Western Avenue on Court Street. In 1871 100 "hands" were working putting out 900 cases of boots and 800 cases of shoes and slippers per year. In 1882 the company ceased operations and Ara Cushman took over the building for his own use, calling it his Cushman Factory #2. This building was in the section that was known as "Railroad Square."

This picture was taken in the Cushco Cafeteria in the Cushman Building. The menu in the background gives the following prices: hamburgers 20¢, cheeseburgers 30¢, grill frankforts 15¢, jello 10¢, milk 10¢, and a piece of pie 15¢. This is believed to be a photograph of the Charles Cushman Company Twenty Year Club, 1953.

This building was an early shoe factory owned by Ara Cushman, which was later remodeled into the Whitehall Hotel. It was located at Court and Railroad Streets, Auburn, also the location of the Eureka Apartments for a period of time. It burned in the 1940s.

The demolition of the Cushman Building. The wooden building was along the railroad tracks from Court Street to School Street. At one time the Cushman Shoe Company was the largest in Maine, and probably in New England. (Auburn Police Deptepartment, 1972.)

The Cushman Shoe Company, c. 1898. Omer Parent (at far right) worked in the Continental Mill and Bates Mill, before working in the Cushman Shoe Shop. He later opened a successful variety store on Ash Street. (The Franco-American Work Experience, L.A. College; photograph by Omer Parents, Sr.)

The Lunn and Sweet Shoe Company, Auburn, February 7, 1913. Among the people in this photograph are, from left to right: (front row) Walter Holmes and Wm. Cliff; (second row) Chas. Ault and Timothy O'Leary; (back row) A.J. Sweet and Ralph Lunn. (Photograph by Washburn.)

The Lunn and Sweet Shoe Shop, Minot Avenue, Auburn. This was the location of the offices.

The Lunn and Sweet Shoe Factory, Minot Avenue, Auburn, in the early 1920s. This is the stitching room where Ralph Cameron was foreman. The wooden box in the front middle of the picture says "New Castle Leather Company."

Lombard's Shoe Shop, Goff Hill, Auburn, 1864. These workers took a break to gather around for a photo session. The shoe shop was located at the junction of Western Avenue and Court Street on the north side of Court Street. The first small shop was started by I.C. Lombard in 1852. By 1864 the shoe shop employed about one hundred people.

Officials and members of the Textile Workers Union of America and the Androscoggin Mill met in 1940 to sign the first textile union contract. From left to right are: Roger Caouette, treasurer of the local union; George Jabar, one of the early labor leaders in Maine; and O'Nues Dube, president of Androscoggin Local 280. Others in the photograph are Louis St. Laurent, Willie Clavet, Valmon Ouellette, Frank Morin, Laurette Hammond, Ovila Brochu (vice-president), Leliane Bosse, Hubert Marcotte, Germaine Berube (shop steward), Clair Fournier Allen, Jackie Lachance Marcotte, Emile Letourneau (shop steward), and George Robin. Signing for the management were Joseph Bussiere (superintendent of the plant) and Albert Lavigne. (From the Franco-American Heritage Collection, L.A. College.)

The office staff of the Packing and Shipping Department of the Bates Manufacturing Company. From left to right are: (front row) Marie Jefferson, Kitty Kane, Bea Ricker, and Ruth Small; (middle row) Margaret Higgins, Louise Harlow, Irene Grondin, Marion Bowker, and Narrine Keene; (back row) Norma Harris, Francis Bussell, and Phyllis Lovewell. This fine group of ladies are standing in front of the Roll of Honor, a list of the employees of the Bates Manufacturing Company serving in the Armed Forces of the United States. (From the Franco-American Heritage Collection, L.A. College.)

The construction of Bates Mill #5, July 16, 1912. The horses are removing gravel in buckets. Notice the lower left umbrella with the following advertising: "Wear Stag Trousers: Union Made Leave Rip." The building on the right in the background houses the Kerrigan Company.

Bates Mill #5, Lewiston, under construction on November 7, 1912.

The dedication of a loom in Bates Mills, Lewiston, 1915. The only two names on the back of the photograph are R.C.C. and Mr. Owen.

The Lewiston Bleachery and Dry Works. It was one of the largest companies for bleaching in the United States. The company was founded by the Franklin Company in 1860. The new boiler house and smoke stack were built around 1890, but were not in use as shown by the smoke coming from two chimneys. In the 1940s the Lisbon Street frontage would be nearly tripled. A new front entrance to the office building and two stair towers were later added. The old "drying sheds" were a memory in 1918. The new City Hall can be seen at the far left. (Photograph by Flagg & Plummer.)

Six

School Days

The Franklin School, Pine Street, Auburn, probably in the spring of 1889 or 1890.

The Webster Grammar School, Auburn, Class of 1896. From left to right are: (front row) Mae Yeaton, Ethal McMurray, Grace Torsey, Frannie Harlow Anna Parker, Lena Stratton, Miss Josephine Cobb (teacher), Mary Stetson, Josiah Williams (principal), Ella Macomber, Miss Margaret Wilson (teacher), Edna Rounds, Alice Smith, Sadie Johnson, Beulah Beal, and Maude Emerson; (middle row) Ruby MacFarland, Herman Burr, Mary Roak, Dana Litchfield, Gertrude DeCoster, Herbert Hersey, Bessie Wood, Herbert Oakes, Maud Stockman, Mae

Carrow, Henry Lowell, Kathleen Robinson, Ralph Blagden, Margaret Peables, unknown,
Florence Grover, unknown, Susie Cook, Percey Haskell, Addie Milligan, and Freed Litchfield;
(back row) Carl White, Arthur Pettengill, Earle Brett, Elmer Greenleaf, Willaim Coan, Karl
Sturgis, Harry Clark, Harold Robinson, Charles Loring, Thomas Chase, and Earle Lyseth.

The Webster School, Auburn, Class of 1938 or 1940.

The fifth grade of the old Webster Grammar School, Auburn, 1913–14. Miss Georgianna Long is the teacher, and the Auburn Library is in the background. From left to right are: (front row) Clarence McIntosh, Merton Spiller, Gauvin McKenzie, Ralph Foss, Bernard Sturtevant, and Kenneth Field; (second row) Madeline Milliken, Catherine Murphy, Florence Adams, Betty Sawyer, Evelyn Taylor, Evelyn Brown, Helen Crossman, Ethel Manning, Vera Damon, Lucy Brenneman, Helen MacFarland, Marguerite Lovett, and Caroline Cushman; (third row) Michael Sullivan, Milton Lyon, Helen Whitney ?, unknown, Hilda Dailey, Eva Gailey, Chester Cox, Lewis Newton, Marion Healey, Audrey Estes, Edward Sawtelle, unknown, and Reuben Ray ?; (back row) Rose Gayton, Mable Cole, Ollie Small, Dorothy Billings, Maude Foss, Beatrice Chase, unknown, Thelma Blaisdell, Claribel Smith, unknown, Elizabeth Sturgis, Charlotte Hunt, Mabel Dearborn, and Irma Atkins.

The Webster School, Auburn, during the spring of 1918. From left to right are: (front row) Carrol Francis, Clayton Field, Stanley Thorpe, Earland Worthing, Kennedy O'Neil, Norton Churchill, Wilbur Veazie, Donald Brown, and Stanley Richardson; (second row) Bertha Thomas, Louis Jones, Harriet Nason, Alice Buchanan, Kathleen Frost, Madeline Kimball, Katherine Cole, Irene Pomeroy, Blanche Pomeroy, and Elizabeth Campbell; (third row) Irvin Verrill, Thurley Giles, Hilda Cleaves, Louise Sawyer, Hazel Pettingill, Elizabeth Ford, Alice Wallingford, Evelyn Kilbreth, Vesta Nason, and Doris Smith; (fourth row) Doris Muller, Constance Whittredge, Athalee Davis, Mildred Steward, David Field, Dana Monk, Kenneth Ryerson, Helen Kenney, Phyllis Forbush, and Eleinor Randall; (back row) Charles Chalimus, Appleton Ford, Donald Tracy, and Alden Littlefield.

The Hotel Road School, Auburn, 1938–39. From left to right are: (front row) Donald Proctor, Charles Barber, Robert Roy, Armand Chabot, Armand Chabot, Richard Mooney, Wilfred LaPointe, and Harry LaPointe; (second row) Durwood Hicks, Marcel Chaliot, Fernard LaPointe, Leonel Dechene, Roger Doyon, George Courbron, and Joseph Barber Jr.; (third row) Shirley Gilbert, Barbara Proctor, Zelma Hicks, Marilyn Chase, Connie Barker, Lucille LaPointe, Joan Pepin, and Loraine Hicks; (back row) Rene Doyon, Terry White, Leau Demers, Elizebeth Demers, Fernard Cote, and Edith Frank Norris. Absent when the picture was taken were Philip LaPointe and Marie Cothram.

The Crowley's School photograph taken March 28, 1928. From left to right are: (front row) Gerald Bussier, Catherine Bussier, Dana Witham, Sylvia Rousseau, Robert Coffin, Antoned Toberge, Laurega Dubois, and Maurice Roberge; (second row) Robert Belanger, Louis Ouiolard, Rosario Bussiere, Alea Dubois, Secil Dubois, Cathaline Roberts, Alfred Belanger, Henry Roberge, Harry Coffin, Louis Seckauski, Neulia Rousseau, and Luciene Bussiere; (back row) Roland Rousseau, Bud Bickford, Anatol ?, Ovelia Bussier, Bussiere Rosario, Dorthy Beaulieura, Antonet LaFlamme, Rupert Car, Isabel Dubois, Stanley Seckauski, Henry Grelrawski, Stanley Giel Gielrawski, William Gielrawski, Abel Rouseau, and Jo Seckauski.

The Crowley Junction School, South Lewiston, Class of 1916. From left to right are: (front row) Omair Saucie, Merle Webber, Orville Hartford, Janie Rohr, Edmond Lemelin, Randolph Frechette, Wallace Witham, and Earl Daten; (middle row) Oliver Lemelin, Lyman Houlten, Bernard Carville, Helen Goff, Nellie Dawes, Marion Witham, and Gilbette Frechette; (back row) Yvonne Lessard, Violette Frechette, Annie Goff, Kenneth Carver, and Miss Murphy.

The Crowley Junction School, South Lewiston, Class of 1910. This was an Edwin H. Washburn photograph. From left to right are: (front row) ? Elwell, ? Elwell, Eddie McKay, Lee Doten, Helen Goff, James McKay, Hazel Adams, William Hartley, Marion Witham, and Janey Hartley; (back row) Alton Cole, Harold Cole, Howard Frost, Cecil Libby, Muriel Cary, Sadie Witham, Dorothy McKay, and Ruth Goff.

Auburn's first school bus, early 1930s. What a big day for these students.

The first grade of the Franklin School, Pine Street, Auburn, 1909–10. Miss Helen Mason is the teacher (Mrs. Leroy Curtis). From left to right are: (front row) Byron Wood, Marguerite Lovett, Doris ?, Elsie ?, Evelyn Brown, Mable Cole, Eleanor Stevens, and Bernard Wood; (second row) Merton Spiller, Verna ?, Helen MacFarland, Madeline Milliken, Florence Adams, Caroline Cushman, and Lila ?; (third row) Clinton Sturtevant, Dorothy Billings, Catherine Murphy, Eleanor ?, Ethel Manning, Charlotte Hunt, and unknown; (fourth row) unknown, Richard ?, Ralph (Gatchell or Bennett), Alton ?, Milton Lyon, and Miss Curtis (teacher); (back row) Kenneth Field, Arthur ?, ? (Neale), Clifford ?, Maurice Davis, and Maurice Snell.

The Park Hill School, Auburn, in the 1890s. The students are as follows, from left to right: (front row) Arthur Whitehouse, Fred Littlefield, Harry Goss, Grace Lunt, Laura Knight, Henry Bennett, and Wil Bennett; (middle row) Gladys Chapman, Annie Woodbury, Gladys Woodman, Ralph Olfene, Hazel Keene, and Charles Harradon; (back row) Arthur Shaw, John Littlefield, Lloyd McFadden, Fannie Bennett, Alice Bennett, and Grace Ingersoll (teacher).

Lewiston High School, Class of 1939. This photograph was taken in front of the Lewiston Armory. (Photograph by Washburn.)

81

The 1893 Lewiston High School football team.

The graduating class of Lewiston High School, June 2, 189?. This is the old high school, opposite Central Maine General Hospital. It looks like the ladies outnumbered the men two to one.

The Edward Little High School football team of 1908. From left to right are: (front row) Radcliff, Earl Kimball, and Theodore Beals; (middle row) Richard, Tibbetts, ? Ward, Ben Isaacson, and unknown; (back row) Sam Caruthers, Loyd McFaddey, Win Carey, Ray March, ? Larrabee, and Robert Sial (principal).

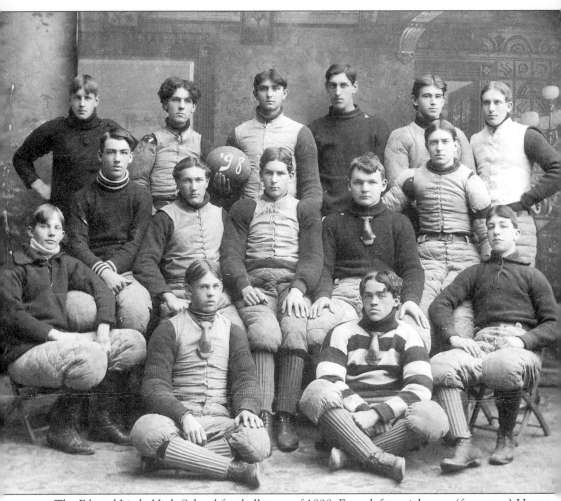

The Edward Little High School football team of 1898. From left to right are: (front row) Harry Clark and Chandler Bearce; (middle row) Herbert Hersey ?, Clarence Drake, Ernest Lord, Wallace Philoon, Marshall Hastings, ? Hodgkins, and Charles Bailey; (back row) Ed Bearce, Eben Harlow, Wallace Clement, Winfield Bearce, ? Lowell, and Henry Hall.

The Edward Little High School basketball team of 1939. From left to right are: (front row) Hood, Haywood, Skinner, and Niles: (back row) Daicey, Couklin, March, and Carey.

The Edward Little High School Editorial Board for the *Oracle*, 1908. From left to right are: (front row) Grace Connor and unknown; (middle row) Alice Estes Atwood, Geoffrey Craig, Ruth Sweetsir, Nathan Harris, and Jessie Alley; (back row) Ray Thayer, unknown, Ray Hayward, Edna Bedell Coombs, Charles Adams, Amy Weeks, and Mellen Pingree.

The Edward Little High School Orchestra 1922–23. From left to right are: (front row) Mariam Skillings, Edna Bolduc, Russell Anderson, Mr. Elbridge Petcher, Arthur Taylor, Harold Dow, Ida Bisbee, and Elizabeth Tighe; (second row) Irma Francis, Hazel Jones, Katherine Johnson, Audrey Estes, unknown, Clayton Taylor, Elaine Stephens, Eva Miller, and Sadie Bornstein ?; (third row) Rae Spaulding, Alden Getchell, Ann Tighe, Sylvia Hoit, Evelyn Chandler, and Francis McCarthy; (fourth row) Lydia Howard, Gerald Newman, Doris Fitz, Wyland Leadbetter, Charlie Jordan, and Charles Siegal; (back row) Henry White, Elwyn Gamage, Helen Merrill, and Archer Jordan.

The Lewiston Normal Training School, Classes of 1910 and 1911. From left to right are: (front row) Rose Doyle, Sadie Berman, Bessie Curtis, Miss. Finch, Mary Leonard, Margaret Dealy, and Sadie Wandtke; (back row) Hazel A. Goss, Carrie Bathey, Rosalie Horne, Helen McDonongh, Helen O'Connor, Elsie Hammond, and Mildred Timberlake. According to the *History of Androscoggin County* (1891), "Unquestionably, this school has had much to do with the present high standard of the Lewiston schools. They are not novices in teaching, for they have had a year's experience, and some of them more, under the instruction of a competent teacher, for this school unites the theory as well as the practice of teaching."

The Maine School of Commerce basketball team of 1929. (Photograph by Tash.)

A 1920s photograph of the early Bates College Gym, behind Nathorne Hall. This building burned to the ground after Bates College constructed their new gym.

A general view of Bates College, Lewiston, taken from "David's Mountain." Bates College grew out of the Maine State Seminary, and the Maine State Seminary sprang from the mind and heart of Reverend Oren B. Cheney, a Free Will Baptist minister in Augusta. In 1854 the buildings at Parsonsfield Seminary, the only Free Baptist school in the state, burned, and Mr. Cheney at once conceived the idea of founding a centrally located school. Benjamin E. Bates of Boston gave a gift of $25,000. In 1863 the name change was made from the Maine State Seminary to Bates College. Bates was the only Free Will College east of Michigan, and in New England there were 30,000 members of that denomination. (*History of Maine* (1919), American Historical Society, Inc.)

Seven
The Twin Cities at Worship and Volunteering

The Bates Street Baptist Church, Lewiston. According to the *History of Androscoggin County* (1891), "This English Gothic Architecture style church was built in 1869–70, and was made with bricks with granite trimmings and pressed brick beltings laid in black cement. This church would seat 800 people, and it cost $ 54,000.00 to build, which included the lot. Situated on Bates St. at the southern extremity of the City Park." Above the altar was written the following words: "How amiable are thy tabernacles, O Lord of hosts!". These words of comfort inspired many church members.

The Clough Meeting House, South Lewiston. According to the *History of Androscoggin County* (1891), "This church consisting of 26 members was organized July 26, 1826. Rev. Messrs Ward, Rev. Lock and Abiezer Bridges took part in the services. The church held its meetings in Aaron Davis's Barn, at the Clough School House and at various private residences in the vicinity until 1846 when the present meeting house was completed. The church had no regular minister for many years, but has maintained worship for the greater part of the time having its pulpit supplied by students from Cobb Divinity School." The South Lewiston Baptist Church met here until they were able to build a new house of worship on Lisbon Road.

Reverend and Mrs. Anthony Lombardi opened up the Clough Meeting House in 1953. This photograph was taken in 1954. The church grew out of the little Clough Meeting House and the church members raised the funds to build a new church building on Lisbon Road. The church eventually changed its name from the Second Baptist Church to the South Lewiston Baptist Church. Reverend Lombardi served this church as the minister for thirty-five years. Reverend Brian Church presently serves as the minister.

Members of the Building Committee of the Second Baptist Church, Lisbon Road. From left to right are Elwood Wing, Fred Chase, Dana Witham, Virgil Thompson, Euphemia Harvey, Roger Barton, Reverend Anthony Lombardi, and Donald Wilson. (Photograph by the *Lewiston Sun*.)

The Hammond Street Methodist Church, Lewiston. In the *History of Androscoggin County* it is noted that the church was organized in June 1870 with fifteen members. The society worshiped in the old Baptist church on Main Street, at the corner of Lisbon Street, until the early part of 1876, when their was church edifice was completed. Mr. Samuel R. Bearce gave the lot, plus $10,000 towards the construction of the new church. The church seated five hundred people, and cost $18,000 to build. (Stereo view published by J.A. McFadden, Bath.)

An Evangelist meeting at the Pine Street Baptist Church, Lewiston. The minister was Merritt L. Gregg, and the evangelist was Waltz ?.

The back of this photograph calls this an "Old-Maids Convention," held at the Pine Street Free Baptist Church, Lewiston. Notice the one man (under the Pinkerton's Electrical Transformer) with twenty-four single ladies. This church broke away from the Main Street Free Baptist Church, Lewiston, on January 3, 1869. They worshiped in the Lewiston Hall until the completion of their house of worship in December 1861 at a cost of $14,000.

The West Danville Free-Will Baptist Church, Marston Corner, Auburn. The church was originally called the Minot, Poland, and Danville Church. It is located at the corner of Beech Hill and Poland Road. Today the church is called the Marston's Corner Baptist Church.

The First Universalist Church, Pleasant Street, Auburn. The Maine Universalist Convention had its origin in a council held June 24, 1828, in the dwelling of James Lowell in Lewiston. Dam Read of Lewiston was the moderator. The second article of the constitution read: "The immoral conduct of any member shall be laid before the society by any rebel of the society knowing the facts. The defendant shall have a fair trial, and for minor offenses may be admonished and forgiven, but for drunkenness, gambling, profanity, or theft he shall be expelled" (*History of Androscoggin County*, 1891).

St. Joseph's Catholic Church, Main Street, Lewiston. In 1867 Saint Joseph's Church was built, making it the first Catholic church in Lewiston. Before that year Lewiston had only Baptist, Methodist, and Congregational churches. The Universalist Society was active during this period. P. McGillicuddy, Esquire, held Catholic services in his home starting in the year 1850. Reverend Charles McCollion, who lived in Portsmouth, New Hampshire, would travel to Lewiston to hold meetings. Father Lucy was the priest that organized the building of St. Joseph's, which was completed at a cost of $55,000.

The St. Peter and St. Paul Catholic Church. The building of this church was a very large project and took four years. The smaller church was torn down in 1905 to make room for the newer and larger building. Fund raising was show to start with, so the church members had to worship in the basement from 1906–30. The dedication speaker was Reverend Joseph Edward McCarthy, D.D., Bishop of Portland.

The Court Street Baptist Church, Auburn, c. 1938–39. Reverend Edward Babcock, D.D., was the minister in the photograph. In the year 1859 some church members from the Lewiston Falls Baptist Church that lived in Auburn decided that a Baptist church in Auburn should be built. They baptized their first member on June 30, 1861. On February 4, 1868, the present lot on Court Street was purchased for $4,000 and a church was built that seated eight hundred people. This new church was dedicated on August 25, 1870.

The Knights of Pythias Hall, 27 Spring Street, Auburn. This was the original meeting place of the present Court Street Baptist Church. This chapel was dedicated on April 6, 1860. The congregation was then known as the Spring Street Baptist Church. It is the property and long-time meeting place of the Eureka Lodge, Knights of Pythias, and of the Pythian Sisters. It has been used as a place of worship by other denominations.

The Court Street Free Will Baptist Church (no longer standing). This Auburn church was organized in 1859. Reverend Arthur Dewitt Paul was the pastor when this photograph was taken in 1916 and he lived at 327 Court Street. Several of the people in this photograph have been identified: (front row, 3rd from left) Harry A. Rand, who worked for the J.P. Hutchinson Insurance Co.; (front row, 2nd from right) Elmer L. Briggs, who owned the J.P. Hutchinson Insurance Co.; (second row, 5th from left) Herbert L. Gatchell; (second row, 10th from left) Louis Flanders; (third row, last man on right) William Briggs; (fourth row, 3rd from left) Arthur French. All others remain unidentified. The church sign now hangs in the Androscoggin Historical Society of Auburn. The church had a seating capacity of eight hundred people.

The Auburn Grange Hall #4 P. of H. This was a very active grange, but is now torn down. The grange was located near Lake Auburn on Route 4.

Auburn Corn Roasters—1889. (Mason Pike Photographers.)

Former Masters of Lewiston's Grange. From left to right are: (front row) Harry White, Walter Scribner, Harry Crowley, Ralph Moyse, Everett Davis, and Bryon Adams; (back row) Errol Houghton, Ralph White, Fred Jordan, Alton Savage, Clayton Hodgkin, Elwin Hodgkin, Irving Hodgkin, and Gordan Mills. (Photograph by Hammond Studio, Chester R. Verrill, Prop., Lewiston.)

The Twin City Indoor Baseball League at the "Ladder Room" in the Auburn Central Fire Station. The date is about 1940. Clockwise around the table, starting at the lower left, are: Howard Nelson, Fred Whirley, Everett Huntley, Carleton Proctor, Walter Pelletier, Willaim Bennett, and Harold Wright (all of Auburn); Paul McGraw, James Donohue, Leo Levesque, Fred Leclair, Albert Moreau, Percy Maguire, Louis Jones, Abner Hodgdon, Eugene Beaudoin, Linwood Edgecomb, Zepherin Drouin, and Gerard Roy (all of Lewiston). In the background is an old horse-drawn hose wagon which was converted to a trailer unit in 1927. It carried a load of 2-and-1/2-inch hose and had a "deck gun" mounted over the hose bed.

This photograph postcard of the Lewiston Grange #2 P. of H., located at Crowley's Junction, South Lewiston, was taken on October 10, 1928. Notice that the entrance was on the side; today the entrance is on the front. Also notice the snow on the ground. Remember, this was taken in October.

The Good Templar's Hall of Crowley's Junction, South Lewiston. The Maine Central Railroad rebuilt this building, because the first building caught fire from a spark that blew off an engine. This hall was where anti-liquor people held their meetings during Prohibition. Before the Good Templar's Hall was at this location, a grocery store, post office, and grain store were located here.

The 28th Annual American Legion Convention, June 21–23, 1946, Lewiston. The 1946 Lewiston American Legion Convention and the members of Lewiston Post #22 welcome guests. From left to right are: (front row) Joseph Pelletier, John Robertson, Martin O'Reilly, Charles Tuttle, and Carl Young; (back row) Gaston Lagrange, Anthony Cormier, Ibra Ripley, Jean Dam, Reginald Ouellette, Patrick Malia, Trefle Caron, and Louis Le Vasseur. Martin L. O'Reilly and Charles I. Tuttle were co-presidents.

The Improved Order of Red Men. This photograph was taken in front of the Androscoggin County Building, Auburn. According to *The History of Maine*, "Prior to the American Revolution, and during the War of 1812, there existed many societies, social and patriotic, known as Sons of Liberty, Red Men, and Tamina Societies. It was the Sons of Liberty, who in 1773, emptied the King's tea into Boston Harbor. Before these societies crystallized, the Improved Order of Red Men came into being. In the 1920's Auburn had 124 members and Lewiston had 94 members." The word "Redmanship" means Americanism. The cardinal principles of the order are Freedom, Friendship, and Charity. One of the greatest works done by the order was caring for orphans in the homes of private citizens. During the 1880s H.G. Foss of Auburn was a Great Chief of the Great Council of Maine. During World War I the National Order of Red Men donated twenty-four ambulances to various government hospitals in the United States.

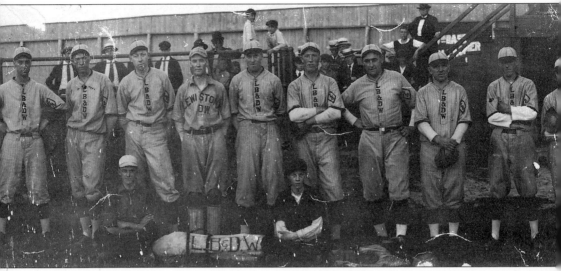

The Lewiston Bleachery and Dye Works baseball team of 1901. From left to right are J. Arthur Cloutier, Tim Driscoll, Bill Cronin, Toby Joyce, Leo Brannigan, Marty Joycee, Tom Breen, Dave Lonergan, Tom Cook, and Joe Cronin. Sitting on ground are Joe Dudzic (left) and Joe Kynotko (right).

Eight
Our People at Work and Play

Engine #1 of the Lewiston Fire Department. The engine was a 1924 American LaFrance 750 G.P.M. Pumper. This 1936 photograph was taken from Bates Street of the old Central Station on Ash Street. From left to right are Rosaire Veerreault, Louis Jones, Percy Maguire, and Ernest Verderber. Paul Guay is on the seat.

The Auburn Fire Department. (Photograph by Washburn Photo.)

A hook and ladder of the Lewiston Fire Department, 1914. The location is the North Bridge over the Androscoggin River.

This picture was taken in 1936 of the Central Fire Station at Ash and Bates Streets, Lewiston. The unit on the left is the William P. Gray Engine #2, and was purchased in 1926. It was named in honor of William P. Gray, who donated $1,000 toward its purchase. The unit on the right is Engine #1, and was purchased in 1924. It was the first motorized pumper owned by the City of Lewiston.

This photograph was taken in the late 1930s on the Bates Street side of the old Central Fire Station, Lewiston. From left to right are Andre A. Roux, Win Davis, and Percy Maguire.

A photograph of firemen taken in front of the DeWitt Hotel, Lewiston. The hotel was located at the intersection of Pine and Park Streets and was constructed c. 1854 by the Franklin Company. The *History of Androscoggin County* reports that "Androscoggin, No. 1 Fire Company was organized on October 26, 1849 in Lewiston. In 1878 the Steamer L. C. Peck # 4 was built by the Amoskeag Company at a cost of $4,250.00. In 1880 the fire-alarm telegraph was installed, and had 27 signal boxes connected to it with 21 miles of telegraph wire."

The officers of the Lewiston Firemen's Relief Association, about 1940. From left to right are: (front row) Ed Lambert, Eugene Bezudoin, Zepherin Crouin, and Percy Maguire; (back row) Dwight B.H. Smith, Wilfred Mailhot, Gerard Roy, Louis Malo, and Emanuel Cote.

The Auburn Fire Station, Court Street. The fire chief is on his white horse. (Photograph by the A.A. Miller Ladder Company.)

The funeral of George "Pa" Whitney. He was the driver of the horse-drawn ladder truck from 1901 to 1919. Hose truck #3 was used as a hearse, and the horses were from the ladder truck. This picture was taken on Turner Street. Mr. Whitney's home was the house on the extreme left. From left to right are: (on the seat) Fred Tuttle and Chief Chester Blethen; (in the back) Carl Spearin, Edgar Finley, and Frank Jackson; (on the side) Carl Allen. (Photograph by Washburn Photo.)

The Auburn Fire Departments' fighting force in the fall of 1932 after the two new white pumpers had been added to the department. From left to right are: (engine #5) Thomas Maguive and James Lawlor; (engine #4) Willis Millett, Ralph Draper, Franklin Prescott, Walter Currier, and Alton Morrell; (hose truck #1) George Small and Thomas Chifelle; (engine #3, on seat) Carl Stretton and Walter Sawtell; (engine #3, on rear seat) John MacDonald, Kenneth Calligan, and Harry Sawyer; (engine #3, on ground) Clarence Handy, Harry Fogg, Mayor Green, and George L. Barnes; (chief's car) councilman ?, City Manager David Walton, and

Councilman Bussiere Ray; (engine #2, on front) Harlan Proctor, Sumner Elwell, and Guy Stewart; (engine #2, on back) Clarence Penley and Patrick Cullinane; (engine #2, on ground) Fred Banks and David Simpson; (ladder #1, on truck) Carlton Proctor, Samuel Towle, Willaim Cross, and Walter Pottle; (ladder #1, on ground) George Cadman; (engine #1, left side, on ground) Warwick Ward; (engine #1, on running board) Elmo Gosselin; (engine #1, on seat) Harold Wright and William Bennett; (engine #1, right side, from top to bottom) Dewey Stephanson, John Magee, and Dexter Knights.

The Engine House of the Auburn Fire Department, 1910, Court Street. From left to right are "Pa" Whitney, unknown, unknown, Sam Towle, John Gould, and Frank Hoydon.

An early 1890s fire engine (L.C. Peck), Auburn, Court Street, across from the YMCA building. It looks like this was a parade.

A c. 1900–1902 photograph of the 1900 Skene Steam Stanhope, the original engine from the steam-driven automobile made in the Rand-Harley machine shop of Lewiston. There were only two made and they were hand-machined. One was for a local doctor and the other was for Mr. Rand himself. The cylinders had a bore of 3-and-1/2-inches while the Stanley engine had a 4-inch bore. The engines developed 800 pounds of steam, and the boiler was hand-made and bound with piano wire. Clarence Rand (on the right) also made the automobiles which the engines powered.

The Maine Central Railroad time-table for the summer of 1871. The time-table gives the following information: "Stage Connections at Auburn daily for North Auburn and Turner. Railroad connections at Danville Junction with the Grand Trunk Railroad. Brunswick for Lisbon and Lewiston." E. Noyes was the Superintendent and L.L. Lincoln was the Assistant Superintendent.

The people in this picture are the owners and employees of the A.L. and E.F. Goss Company which was located at the head of Lincoln Street near Main Street. The photograph was taken in Brunswick when the group was on its way to an outing near the ocean. Al Goss is on the left of the group, and Tom Slater is on the right. Behind the group is a Merrymeeting Electric Car.

The Lewiston-Brunswick Trolley Barn, Lisbon Street, Lewiston. Before electric trolleys came into being trolley cars were pulled by horses. A group of men from Massachusetts and New York formed the L.-A. Horse Railroad Company in 1881. By the early 1890s the company employed 30 people, owned 90 horses, and had laid 14 miles of track. The State Employment Building now stands on this location.

These unknown railroad men are busy at work keeping the area in top shape.

Engine #274, Lewiston Station. The railroad men in the photograph are, from left to right: P. Poulin; breakman Paipon Peverly; (at the cab window) Al Soule; (on the steps) Ed Finley; and breakman Harvey Dow. (Photograph by Washburn Photo.)

The Waseca Club baseball team, Auburn, 1910. From left to right are: (front row) Norman Litchfield, Arthur Beede, Gus Fortier, Elmer Dennis, and Alfred Wantke; (second row) Clarence Stockbridge, Eben Talcott, Harry Goss, William Skinner, and Ray Thayer; (third row) Hebert Gammon, Forest Atwood, George Desaulniers, Ralph Cobb, Max Linscott, and Elmer Daicy; (back row) Lyman Bearce, Merton Warren, Harry Wormwood, and Roy Hamilton.

Marshall's old-fashioned popcorn truck, Auburn. This was a model "A" Roadster, and though you could find it originally at different locations in Auburn, most people remember the days that Arthur Francis Marshall sold popcorn on Turner Street, Auburn. He started selling popcorn in 1907. He died at the age of eighty, and his nephew Robert operated the popcorn truck until the 1970s.

This was ex-Governor Dingley's residence in Lewiston. Dingley was a leading figure in Lewiston and around the state. As governor he signed the bank charters for the Manufacturer's National Bank and the People's Savings Bank. He also was treasurer of Squirrel Island (off Boothbay Harbor). *The History of Maine* states "Feb. 1865 it became the duty of the Maine Legislature to act on the thirteenth amendment to the constitution abolishing slavery. The Legislature had already passed a resolution introduced by Nelson Dingley of Lewiston favoring such an amendment. After the vote Dingley proposed the assemblage unite in singing the grand old doxology OLD-HUNDRED. It was sung with spirit and tears."

The Auburn Trust Company, located between the Elm Hotel and the Oscar Jones Drug Store, which was on the corner of Court and Main Street. This photograph was probably taken before 1902 since the building was purchased by Auburn Savings that year. The officers of the bank were Samuel F. Merrill (president), George C. Wing (vice-president), and James F. Atwood (treasurer). Notice the sign on the right advertising the Auburn Public Library, which was located in rooms upstairs. Another sign states that there are "rooms to let." The banks offered "Bonds, Investment Securities, and Safe Deposit Vaults." The arched driveway on the left lead to a rear lot owned by the Elm Hotel.

The city of Auburn's mail carriers. The post office was located at the Morrill-Webber Building. William W. Casey is at the top left. The other men include Harry H. Keene, Ernest C. Lane, William E. Quimby (second from right), Wallace I. Gowell, Hector O. Lafayette, Fred D. Miller (third from left), and Harold W. Spafford. The year is uncertain, but there is a date of 1911 on the back of the photograph. In 1887 Auburn numbered the houses and started home delivery. In the 1830s a letter cost $2 to be mailed from Augusta to Lewiston, and Edward Little of Auburn owned this route for a period of time. On July 15, 1799, Lewiston became the second city in the area to establish a post office.

The *Lewiston Journal* composing room, February 9, 1886. Note the setting of the type by hand. (Photograph by Worthley and Owen.)

An Auburn bankers baseball game at the Lewiston Park, c. 1905. From left to right are: (front row) William Greenleaf of the National Shoe and Leather Bank, and Bernard Chase of the Auburn Savings Bank; (back row) Horace Day of the First National Bank, Auburn; Mr. Stetson of Auburn's Mechanics Savings Bank; Linwood E. Ashton, Chester Miller, and Wesley Day, all of the First National Bank; and Willis Atwood and R.E. Smith of the National Shoe and Leather Bank.

The Shoe and Leather Bank building, Court and Turner Streets, Auburn. The bank was organized in February 1875. When the bank started it used part of the Mechanics Savings Bank in Auburn's Hall Block. In 1889 both banks moved into another new building which they shared for twenty-one years. Then the Shoe and Leather Bank built this new building. Ara Cushman was the first president and John T. Randall was the first vice-president. The Mechanics Savings Bank of Auburn was a major stockholder in this bank. A funeral parlor and apartments were located at the far left. You could have a lunch at a small lunch room located on the first floor to the right of the photograph. The building was razed in the 1970s.

The Class of 1926, graduating from the School of Nursing, St. Mary's General Hospital, Lewiston. The Sisters of Charity of St. Hyacinthe, a religious order arriving in Lewiston in 1878, founded and later began the School of Nursing in 1908. The School of Nursing provided many Franco-American women the opportunity to pursue a career in nursing. This photograph is from the archives of The Society of Sisters of Charity of St. Hyacinthe. (The Franco-American Work Experience, L.A. College.)

The Central Maine General Hospital, Lewiston. Miss Lamberson and Miss R. Metcalfe were two nurses who worked at the CMGH in 1912. According to *Androscoggin County Art Work* (1893), "The first physician to settle in Lewiston was Dr. Joel Wright in 1776, and during the 1890's there were twenty resident practitioners, enough, certainly, to look well after the general health of the people." Dr. Wright was a botanical physician and lived on what is now Eastern Avenue. He died on July 26, 1821.

The First Red Cross Volunteers of Auburn and Lewiston. From left to right are: (first row) Miss Annia Wiseman, Mrs. C.W. Lawlor, Miss Hazel Mitchell, Miss Annia Brawshaw, Mrs. Iva Safford, Mrs. F.H. Packard, Mrs. C.C. Peaslee, Mrs. Hattie Allen, and Miss Therma Hicks; (back row) Mrs. Charles Bosehby, Mrs. Ashley Thurston, Mrs. Merton Warren, Mrs. John McMurrey, Mrs. F.A. Jones, Miss Lerona A. Chaplin, Mrs. A.W. Auehowy, and Miss Helen McCaretry. This photograph is dated 1918. (Photograph by Harry L. Plummer, Lewiston.)

Auburn and Lewiston doctors and dentists. From left to right are: (front row) Edward P. Pierce, Wallace Webber, W. Renwick, Peasly, Smell, John Sturgis, B.G.W. Cushman, and Barrell; (second row) Joe Seanall, E. Call, Andrews, Randall, Higgin, Leavitt, Wm. Bolster, and Al. Grant; (third row) G. Twaddle, Julius Gotlieb, Pendleton, H. Miller, Sam Sawyer, Wm. Fahey, Edson Buner, and Arch Jordan; (back row) unknown, unknown, R. Goodwin, Cunningham, Dupras, John Cartland, and Carlton Rand. The date of this photograph is unknown.

119

The old Read House, Lewiston. This house was built by Daniel Read in 1802, and his family was one of the first families to settle in Lewiston. Daniel and Lemuel Read built this large square in 1802 on the farm they bought from Samuel Robinson at the old Ferry Way, below the Porter Mill. Daniel served as Lewiston's first postmaster for forty years.

Dr. Clement's office was located at 374 Lisbon Street, Lewiston. He was one of the many physicians trained in Quebec who came to Lewiston to serve the immigrants from Canada and their children. Twelve physicians grouped themselves into a French-speaking medical society. Notice the advertising in the windows for "Kohler's One Night Corn Cure, Sanital Tooth Powder." (The Franco-American Heritage Collection, L.A. College.)

Erlon Dingley of the Dyer Road, Lewiston, with Ralph White and Fred ?. They are gathering the apples during the fall harvest.

The Upper Maine Central Railroad Station was a favorite place to have a photograph taken. From left to right are: (front row) Roger Allarie, Arlene Carbone, Phyllis Alexandar, and Clifford Burnham; (back row) Mrs. Allarie, Julist Allarie, Olive Carbone, and Pat LaRivieve.

"Fire Destroys Field Bros.-Gross Building; 3 Alarms Sounded, 5 Departments Fight Blaze." As a dramatic touch to the second day of Fire Prevention Week, this spectacular blaze drew thousands of spectators to the scene. (*Lewiston Evening Journal*, October 9, 1945.)

A peg shop, East Auburn. The man at the window is Alexander Berry, who rebuilt the Gulf Island Dam. The man at the door, near the gatehouse, is ? Ersking, Jim Clark's boss. The municipal beach is off to the right..

This birthday party was held at Dr. Lenard's home on Dyer Road in Lewiston. Dr. Lenard was a professor at Bates College. This party was held on Friday, April 31, 1934. Several of the children in the photograph are from the White family (Ilda, Pauline, Dora, Betty, Mae, and Don).

A reunion party at the Mirimar Tea Room, Lion's Club, Young's Corner, Auburn, Maine. This reunion happened on October 19, 1957. From left to right are: (first row) Mabel Eaton, Gertrude Stetson, Mrs. Fred Poole (Grace Mower Eames), Mrs. Pray (Arlie Beals), Mrs. Atwood (Alice Estes), Mrs. Rowe (Marie Willis), Mrs. Lancaster (Amy Bartlett), Clara Butler, Mrs. Roland Whitehouse (in a Wallingford), Roland Whitehouse, Fred Wentzel, Mrs. Mabel Boothby, Edna Cornforth, Mrs. McCarthy (Francis Johnson), Mrs. Sweetsir, Mrs. Oakes, Margaret Dick, and host Russell S. Smith; (second row) Margaret Cassilly, Mrs. Chester Hutchinson (Gladyse McMurray), Mrs. Barton (Virginia Babcock), Lulu Emery, Ann Bonnar, Mrs. Vining (Margaret Wilson), Mrs. Harmon (Evelyn Winship), Mrs. Record (Althea Winship), Mrs. Day (Estelle Humphries), Nellie Cook, Lena Cook, Mrs. McKinney (Lona Tarr), Edith Dunn, Mrs. Wallingford (Winneford Olfene), Alma Tuttle, Mrs. Wells (Ethel Stephens), Mrs. Elmer Gerrish (Edna Woodward), and Mrs. Philoom (Alice Rowe); (third row)

Mrs. Kefferstan (Anna Dick), Blanche Smith, Mrs. Russell (Virgie Harris), Mrs. Burnham (Etta Miller), Mrs. Irish (Grace Dana), Mrs. Franklin Prescott, Mrs. Dwinal (Genevieve Dwinal), Mrs. Cartland, Mrs. Storah (Maude Prescott), Maurice McCarthy, Ira Waterman, Raymond Oakes, Elmer Gerrish, Lucian French, Ray Thayer, William Skinner, Karl Toner, Dan Stetson, Mrs. Marshall Charles Marshall, Harold Spofford, Mrs. Rawstron (Hazel Arris), and Mrs. Skinner; (fourth row) Mrs. Bailey (Lora Swift), Mrs, Norman Litchfield (Evelyn Plummer), Mrs. Karl Toner, Mrs. Packard (Bertha Hasty), Mrs. Ashton (Iva Libby), George Akers, Mrs. Hunt, Guy Fitz, Norman Litchfield, John Libby, Wilber Burnham, Olaf Dwinal, James Philoon, George Barton, Erlan Irish, George Bearce, Robie Libby, and Carl Monk; (back row) Fred Poole, Herman Sweetsir, Richard McKinney, Ralph Rowe, Claude Packard, Merton Vining, Herbert Gammon, Linwood Bailey, Bancroft Wallingford, Forrest Atwood, Lester Hunt, and Tom Storah.

The steamer *Lewiston*, also called the *Frank A. Hale*, Lake Auburn, most likely at the North Auburn Landing. The captain of this steamer from 1885 to 1886 was F.R. Whitney. Do you remember those breath-taking moonlight cruises on Lake Auburn? The steamer *Lewiston* was a great evening for you and that special person in your life.

The Auburn-Lewiston Airport, Auburn. This was a hanger on the Old Hotel Road side of the Auburn-Lewiston Airport. The hanger was built by the WPA in 1939–40. The airplane on the left is a bi-plane owned by Henry Dingley of Auburn. The airplane on the right is a Piper "J-3" Cub.

Pee-Wee the Boston Bull Dog is standing next to an old glass milk jug. Remember when milk was delivered right to your door? Pee-Wee belonged to Marion W. Hinkley of Lewiston.

Acknowledgments

I have enjoyed this research project, and I hope this book will help you walk through the pages of history in our Twin Cities.

Someone once wrote "the peasant may be able to labor without a library, but not the exegete." I want to pay special tribute to Robert Taylor, Executive Secretary of the Androscoggin Historical Society, Auburn. Mr. Taylor is a historian who takes his work seriously. I want to thank Dr. Madeleine Giguere of the Franco-American Heritage Collection, Lewiston and Auburn College, Lewiston. I also want to thank Barbara McIntosh, Librarian of the *Lewiston Sun-Journal*, and the personnel of the Lewiston and Auburn Libraries.

Beyond the written resources and collections, this research project relies heavily on many years of discussion of the culture and history of Androscoggin's Twin Cities. To the countless people no words of thanks are adequate to express the debt that is owned to them. Most of all I want to express my serious appreciation to my wife Patricia, because she proofread and help me put the book together. I want to thank our two children who are still at home, David and Melissa, for their patience when I had publishing deadlines to meet. Our oldest son Timothy and our daughter-in-law Julie were always a source of encouragement.

I want to formally express my gratitude to my parents, Harold and Arlene Dutille; my grandmother, Olive Carbone; and my wife's parents, Dana and Ilda Witham, for all the historical photographs and information they provided. Special thanks goes out to Lemeul and Frances Stinson for those special photographs they provided.